The
Little Book
of

The little Book of Kids' Talk

NANETTE NEWMAN

EBURY PRESS
LONDON

5 7 9 10 8 6 4

© Bryan Forbes Ltd 1999

First published in the United Kingdom in 1999 by Ebury Press
Random House · 20 Vauxhall Bridge Road · London SW1V 2SA

Random House Australia (Pty) Limited
20 Alfred Street · Milsons Point · Sydney · New South Wales 2061 · Australia

Random House New Zealand Limited
18 Poland Road · Glenfield · Auckland 10 · New Zealand

Random House South Africa (Pty) Ltd
Endulini · 5A Jubilee Road · Parktown 2193 · South Africa

Random House UK Limited Reg. No. 954009

A CIP catalogue record for this book is available from the British Library

ISBN: 0 09 182536 9

Designed by Lovelock & Co

Printed and bound in the UK

love is important
becaus if people did
not love each other
there wouldn't
be any people.

Lynn aged 7

I think love is borring,
people only do it when they
have lots of time off.

Una aged 10

you can only love
things near you,
you can't love
countries or
lots of peopl

Rose aged 6

I sometimes think
I love everything and
Everybody But I know
I don't

Soraya aged 9

You couldn't make
everyone in the world
Love each other.
They dont even get
on in blocks of flats.

Lois aged 7

you should never
love someone you
dont like much

Katy aged 7

If only the
world were
made of love

Louise aged 7

sex is a part
of love but not
a very good part.

Joanna aged 6

Love is hard to do to peeple you don't perticularly like.

Deborah aged 10

Me Dad went to
prison and we have
to keep remembring
to love him

Jean aged 7

Love it makes you
coff a lot

Peter aged 5

my aunty falls
in love when we
go on holiday but she
never likes it
and she cries

Leonard aged 6

I once saw some one
fall in love In a car.
It wasn't going though.

Sally aged 7

I saw my sister fall
out of love it was
very interesting

David aged 8

A man fell in love
with my auntie
on a train but she
pulled the cord and
he stoped.

Liz aged 6

you have a hart
attak if you fall
in love to kwickly

Paul aged 7

if I was god I would
go to all the countries and
say love each other and
stop being greedy

Raj aged 9

Lots of people say they love children but mostly they're cross with them.

Vivien aged 11

My friend says
kissing is worse
than haveing flu.

Caroline aged 6

why do all those
fhootballers kiss each
other on the Telly.
They're not married
they're not
even engaged,

Jason aged 6

I shall see how I like
being marrid and if
I dont like it I will
try sumthing else

Mark aged 11

MY sister only wants
to get married
because she's a
rotten show off.

Peter aged 9

It is silly to get Married before you are 12

Edward aged 6

I dont like to see old ladies and men getting married becaus theyre to old for it

Dino aged 6

My brother didn't
want to get married
He wanted to take
me to football

Caroline aged 6

my brother got
married he didnt
fall in love
he just wanted
some one older
to talk to

Theo aged 7

I went to my uncles wedding but I got sick so I don't suppose he'll ask me to his next one

Mario aged 6

I think you can fall
in love if you have
your picture taken in
frunt of the church.

Eric aged 5

Some people
have babies
just buecause
their friends
say they shud

Naomi aged 8

it is easier to have
a baby if you
a cat

Tricie aged 6

first of all you get
in love get married
and get a baby or
you can do it the
other way round

Peter aged 9

To have a baby
the Mother has
to lay an egg
then the mail
cracks it.

Alison aged 8

you can't talk about
babies being made
until you are in
the 4th form

Davina aged 10

I don t know how
a baby gets there and
I think Id rather
be serprized.

Claire aged 8

Some babies dont
Want to be born but
there is nothing they
can do ab.out it

David aged 6

If you want to
have a baby go
to the library

Pierre aged 8

You mustn't giv
Yoew born bady
Sweets its a waste.

Lisa aged 4

Some babys come out
in nighties and boots

Juliet aged 4

My sister came out too
early so she lived in a
glass house for 3 weeks

Jake aged 5

🦋

my mum only likes
little babies. when they
get old like me. she
smacks them.

Ronald aged 5

My brother looked horrible
when he was born but I didn't
say so because they wouldn't
let me change him

Leigh aged 6

You should n't
have babies on
Sunday because
God wants
you to rest.

Merino aged 7

You should never
hit a baby because
it can't hit back

Mike aged 6

when you are a baby
you can see your
mummys bosum but
when you grow up its
not alowed and I
think thats a silly rule

Vivienne aged 6

You have to love
your own baby
because everyone else
finds them a
newsance.

Patrick aged 8

when you are a baby
your mother feeds you
from her bozom but
she can only do milk

Felicity aged 7

You shoud never help
a baby to walk becaus.
It falls down and cuts
its knee and you
always get a smack.

Cormac aged 8

A baby duznt know
how to be norty.
It has to be tort.

Rosalie aged 7

when I grow up I
shall have lots of
babis, then I'll get
married and live
happily ever after

Lisa aged 6

Mary had Jesus so that she could get a house

Christine aged 6

The 3 kings gave
Jesws nasty
Christmas presents

Loise aged 6

people like to
have babies
for christmas

Anne aged 4

theres nothing
in the Bible
about sending
christmas Cards

David aged 8

I think Jesus would be upset if he ~~knew~~ knew what went on at Christmas!

Anthea aged 11

Everybody loves baby
Jesus even my uncle and
both my bruthers but I
don't. I love the three
wizmen best becus they
broat presense.

John aged 5

Once I saw a
Christmas tree
being put to death

Sally aged 8

God is wonderful he.
maked the holi world
and he maked us all

Huw aged 6

its not fair to blame
god for everyth-ing
becaus he cant answer back

Ruba aged 10

I Wish god had ritten
the Bibel so that
evryone coold
understand it

Jean aged 10

God should bless
<u>ALL</u> little children.

Sandra aged 8

I think god made
two many peeple

Eric aged 7

Good pepul always friten bad pepul

Mark aged 7

I don't think there
should be Rich
churches when there
Are poor people

Fiona aged 11

When you go to church
you put mony in the
box and god loves you

Florence aged 7

Jesus wanted people
to be happy but
he didnt tell them
how to do it

Naomi aged 8

Some people go on too
much about being
happy so everybody
wants to be it all
the time and they
cant so they get sad

Adrian aged 8

I dont think you
know you hav been
happy until youre not

Mark aged 11

OLd ladys arentreeLy
oLd Ladys. Therejust
pepel waringold
clobhes.

Jamie aged 6

I don't know when you get old but I expect it's when you can't run any more

Rosalind aged 5

When old people go
on holiday they
sit on deckchairs and
wish they hadnt come

Amy aged 8

Old people and
children need to be
loved more than
those inbetween.

Anna aged 10

old people read
to you until they
fall asleep

Craig aged 6

if you get old to qweekly you never groo up

Winston aged 5

I hayt scool and scool
lunches and the
teecher and all my
friends

Patrick aged 6

Our school cook
is a Secret
Poisoner

Sam aged 10

My best friend is gradually becoming a brown person from India

Jane aged 6

My best enemy is mark.

David aged 6

I woodnt like
me as a frend
becorse I tell fibs.

Ann aged 7

My friend wants to
run away but he doesn't
know where to go.

Tarmin aged 7

My father has a cros
face in the holedays

Jean aged 7

every body you meet
on holiday are nicer
then when you
meet them at home

Harriet aged 9

my daddy shouts
when he speaks a
foregn language
he doesn't know

David aged 10

theres not much
~~room~~ on the moon
not even a nice beach

Andrew aged 7

I went swimming but my body kept wanting to drown.

Jim aged 7

when I was on holiday
in France I ate a lot
of rhineoserous.

Clare aged 6

I can speak French.
I can say Paris.

Jane aged 5

My granny doesn't wear tights because once she fell over.

Elizabeth aged 5

My sister says she
eats men alive
but shes only
pretending.

Mandy aged 6

My Uncle is a riligous
Maniac but I think
he has another job
as well.

Stephen aged 6

my brother cant work
because hes old.
hes 21.

Camela aged 8

Your parents
have to tell you
off because they
don't want you to
grow up like them

Simon aged 10

When my mummys
cross she talks
with a Nasty
smack in Her voice

Victoria aged 5

Mothers and other nasty people frighten children to make them be good

Ben aged 6

My dad sais he's
reading the news
but he's only
looking at ladies
with no clothes on.

Tim aged 10

My Granny was
a sufferer jet
I think she flew
a lot

Robert aged 7

my Sister and brother
tell lyes it runs in
the family

Laura aged 5

My big sister has
gone To pot and
prison

Enid aged 6

I've got three daddys
which is nice at birthdays
but not at other times

Elena aged 5

My mummy and
Daddy dont love
each other they
only love me

Layla aged 8

My Granny cries when she's happy and when she's sad she just stares.

Davina aged 10

My Grann is in love with the pope but he's never goin to marry

Richard aged 6

My dad likes   white people
black people chinese people
but not people from
Tottenham.

Albie aged 7

traffic wardens have
to be cross all day ells
they lose there jobb.

Tim aged 6

If a traffic warden
sees you kissing in a car
you get cramped

Alice aged 6

My dad says you must never hate anyone except traffic wardens.

Andrew aged 8

If you're a nurse
you have to be
dessicated.

Sophie aged 6

I will be a
teecher and get long
holidays

Richard aged 6

when I grow up I
will be a doctor
and pull things out
and put things back

Linda aged 5

Our doctor sais this wont hurt while its <u>hurting</u>

Christine aged 7

I bit my doctor
when I was little but
it didn't hurt

Katy aged 4

Even nasty
people are nice

when you're ill

Marcus aged 8

I think when you vote you have to do it in private. Its like swearing

Jill aged 7

politicians are

people Sometimes

Alison aged 9

Politicians are people who tell
other people to go to war

Anthony aged 13

I bet if animals had votes they'd vote we didn't eat them

Carole aged 6

A prime minister is so busy he doesn't have time to think

Bruce aged 8

Jesus could have been a pri minister if hed wanted to

Veronica aged 7

My Friend says my
dad is a red but he
isn't he's a bus driver

Alex aged 7

If I had a vote.
I'd vote for the
christmas Party

Sandra aged 6

Id vote to stop
wars but they
Never ask you that

Mary aged 7

My auntie took
me to the zoo
and we saw too
politishuns

Katy aged 5

My daddy says he votes to go to the pub every night.

John aged 7

My dad works at
being a striker and
when I grow up I
shall work there as well

George aged 6

I went to the house
of Lords once, to
watch the English
play the Australians

Kevin aged 8

I wish they wouldn't
Tax my daddy because
it always makes
him cross with me.

Robert aged 6

To get a vote you
hae to kiss old
women and babies
and that spreads
deseese

Katrina aged 7

politicians wave
a lott when they
tell you bad news

Elena aged 9

Why can't you
vote for Love?

Brenda aged 8

I never watch
polliticks there
two dangerus

Rhodrey aged 5

When you grow up and
get a job the politicians
make you pay for
their taxis.

John aged 8

It doesn't
matter what
you believe
in as long as you
believe in
something

Rosemary aged 12

My dog had
lots of babies when
he was young but
when he got old
he jus bit people

Martin aged 7

MY CAT HATES
BABIES BECAUSE
THEY DRINK HIS MILK

Cathy aged 6

It's no good taking your dog to a wedding because they don't like Singing.

Martha aged 6

my sister Keeps biting
our Dog

Peter aged 6

When you know my hedgehog he has a wonderful personality.

Emma aged 10

MY TORTUS FELL IN LOVE BUT
IT MADE HIM TIRED AND HE WENT
TO BED FOR ABOUT FOUR YEARS.
I THINK LOVE DOES MAKE YOU
TIRED, SPECIALLY OLD WOMEN.
THEY ALLWAYS SLEEP A LOT.

John aged 6

I wish they
Could Declare love
Instead of War.

Deirdre aged 11

Sometimes when theres
lots of war they
ration love.

Tessa aged 8

I wish Jesus would come
back and stop the fighting
because I think they've
all had enough by now.

Alan aged 7

When you go to heaven you have to say sorry to the holy gost for not beleeving in him.

I dont beleeve in gosts so Im not goin there.

Kim aged 7

when my sister
was born she
decided to go straight
back to heaven.

Lucinda aged 5

They give you a lovely party when you die.

Jamie aged 6

When your ~~dedo~~ dead people
tarlk about you alot.

Tracy aged 7

You have to have
a funeral so that God
knows your Coming.

Astra aged 9

I went to my gran's
funeral to see her elated

Gavin aged 8

It's sad for
cows Because
they're a swear word.

Sam aged 6

all my clothes
have had other

people in them

Paolo aged 7

When I put my new
coat on my hands were
hiding

Diana aged 5

I want to dance but my feet won't let me.

Sandra aged 6

I ran away but nobody came to find me so I ran Back.

Mela aged 7

I hate spoilt
children because
they have everything
I want.

David aged 8

I don't like eating
dead oranges

Emma aged 4

I've been growing up
all day

Emma aged 4

The Little Book
of
Kids' Talk